Break It Down

How Scientists Separate Mixtures

by Jonathan Curley and Ashley Chase

SEEDS
OF SCIENCE

ROOTS
OF READING®

Published and Distributed by

Delta Education
...because children learn by doing.®

A member of
School Specialty
Science

Published and Distributed by

Delta Education
...because children learn by doing.®

A member of
School Specialty
Science

These materials are based upon work partially supported by the National Science Foundation under grant numbers ESI-0242733 and ESI-0628272. The Federal Government has certain rights in this material. Any opinions, findings, and conclusions or recommendations expressed in this material are those of the author(s) and do not necessarily reflect the views of the National Science Foundation.

Developed at Lawrence Hall of Science and the Graduate School of Education at the University of California at Berkeley

Seeds of Science/Roots of Reading® is a collaboration of a science team led by Jacqueline Barber and a literacy team led by P. David Pearson and Gina Cervetti.

Delta Education LLC
PO Box 3000
Nashua, NH 03061
1-800-258-1302
www.deltaeducation.com

Break It Down: How Scientists Separate Mixtures
594-0073
ISBN: 978-1-59821-547-2
Printing 2 – 7/2011
Standard Printing Company, Canton, OH

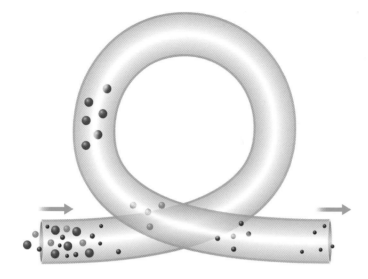

Contents

Milk may not look like it's a mixture, but it is.

Most Matter Is Mixed

You are all mixed up. We don't mean you are confused. We mean that you are a **mixture** of thousands of different **substances**.

You're not alone. Most **matter** is mixed. Almost everything in the world is a mixture of different substances. A substance is something that's made of only one kind of **atom** or **molecule**, such as gold or water. We don't often find substances on their own in nature. They are almost always part of a mixture.

These **models** show a few of the different kinds of molecules that make up milk.

water molecule

protein molecule

sugar molecule

fat molecule

Think of milk. Milk may look like a pure substance, but it's not—milk is a mixture. There is no such thing as a milk molecule. Milk is a mixture of water molecules, protein molecules, sugar molecules, fat molecules, and more.

Apple juice is also a mixture of molecules, including water molecules, sugar molecules, and **acid** molecules. Paint, tears, and **liquid** soap are all mixtures, too.

Not all mixtures are liquids. Rocks, soil, bricks, and many other **solids** are mixtures. Even **gases** can be mixtures. The air on Earth is a mixture of oxygen and other gases.

In some mixtures, such as this rock, you can see the different parts.

In other mixtures, such as this apple juice, you can't see the different parts.

Soil is a natural mixture.

Scientists Break Mixtures Down

People make some mixtures, such as paint and brick, but most mixtures are not made by people. They are just naturally mixed together. Scientists often want to break these mixtures down into parts. Why? Breaking a mixture down can help scientists understand it better.

Paint is a mixture made by people.

When scientists break a mixture down, they can find out what substances are in the mixture. That can help scientists **identify** the mixture, or figure out what it is.

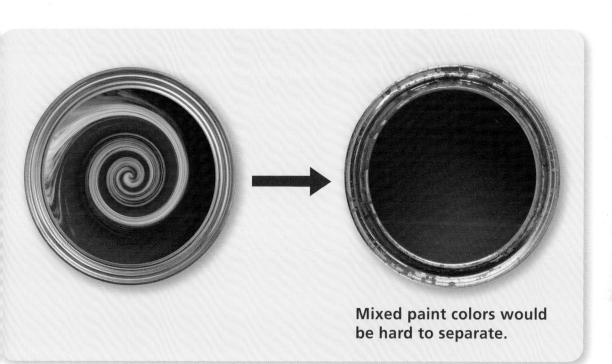

Mixed paint colors would be hard to separate.

Breaking a mixture down can also make it more useful. Sometimes a scientist wants to use just one part of a mixture. Scientists separate a mixture into its parts to get the part they want.

Mixtures can be hard to separate. Mixing two different colors of paint together is easy, but how could you separate the colors once they were mixed? That would be much harder to do.

This book looks at three mixtures and how scientists break each mixture down.

Break It Down to Solve Problems

Most of the water on Earth is in the ocean. Ocean water is a mixture of water and different kinds of salt. It is much too salty for people to drink.

In some parts of the world, there is very little water for drinking. Making salty ocean water safe to drink helps people in places where drinking water is hard to find. However, the water must be separated from the rest of the mixture.

This city is in a desert that is next to the ocean. Drinking water for the city comes from separated ocean water.

Water and salt have different **properties**. Properties are things about matter that people can see, feel, smell, hear, taste, or measure. Water molecules are smaller than many other kinds of molecules. Scientists have figured out how to use this property to separate pure water from the salty ocean water mixture.

Ocean water is pumped through pipes. The mixture of water and salt is pushed through a filter. The filter has holes in it that are much too small to see. Tiny water molecules are small enough to pass through the filter, but the atoms that make the water salty remain trapped. Only pure water comes out on the other side of the filter, and this water is safe for people to drink.

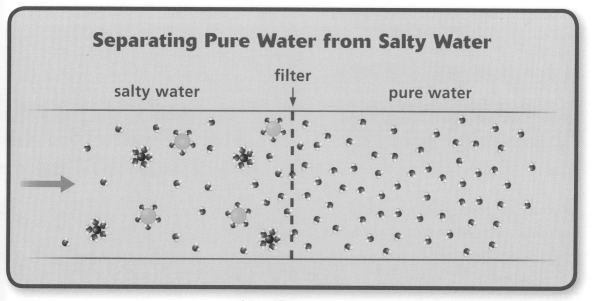

Separating Pure Water from Salty Water

salty water   filter   pure water

This **diagram** shows how the water can be separated from a mixture of water and salt, using a kind of filter.

Blood is
a mixture.

Break It Down to Save Lives

Blood is a mixture, and different parts of blood do different things. Some parts of blood help fight off sickness. Other parts help make a scab so that a cut stops bleeding.

Plasma is the liquid part of blood. It lets blood flow through the body. It also has important proteins that help keep the body healthy.

People give blood so that the plasma and other parts of blood can be used to save lives.

Sometimes a person who is sick or hurt needs extra plasma. This plasma comes from blood that people have given to help others. To get the plasma, scientists must separate it from the other parts of the blood.

Scientists use the properties of the different parts of blood to separate the mixture. Plasma has the property of being liquid at room **temperature**. The other parts of blood are solid at room temperature.

To separate blood, scientists use a machine called a **centrifuge**. A centrifuge separates the parts of blood by spinning the blood very fast. How does a centrifuge do this? Think of spinning around on a tire swing. It feels like you are pulled outward as the swing spins. The same thing happens to the blood in a centrifuge.

The blood in this tube has been separated by a centrifuge. The plasma is the yellow part at the top.

The centrifuge holds tubes of blood that are arranged in a circle. The centrifuge spins around. This spinning separates the solid parts of blood from plasma, the liquid part of blood. The solid parts end up farther from the center of the centrifuge. The liquid plasma ends up closer to the center. The separated plasma can be used to help people who are sick or hurt. Separating mixtures can save lives!

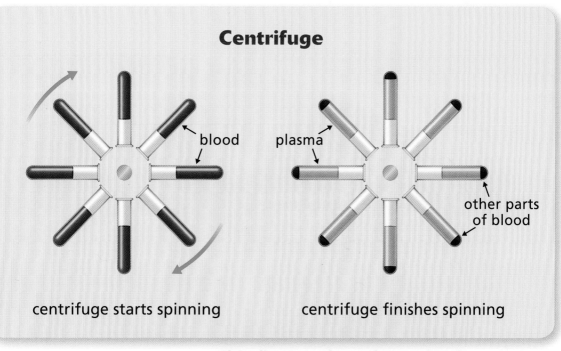

Centrifuge

blood   plasma

other parts
of blood

centrifuge starts spinning   centrifuge finishes spinning

This diagram shows how scientists separate blood by spinning it in a centrifuge.

Scientists found a strange mixture inside ancient pots buried deep underground.

Break It Down to Uncover the Past

Breaking a mixture down can help scientists identify it. Scientists found ancient pots buried deep underground. Inside the pots was a brown mixture. The scientists thought the mixture might be food left over from a great feast. They wanted to identify the mixture to learn about the foods people ate more than 2,700 years ago.

The scientists could not use sight and smell to identify the mixture. The mixture was very old. It no longer looked and smelled the way it had when it was fresh. The scientists needed other kinds of **evidence**. They decided to find out what molecules the mixture was made of. To do this, they used gas **chromatography**.

Like a centrifuge, gas chromatography uses the properties of different parts of a mixture to separate the mixture. Gas chromatography can separate the substances in a mixture by the size of their molecules.

This is how gas chromatography works: Scientists take a little bit of a solid or liquid mixture and heat it until it boils. This makes the mixture turn to gas. The gas mixture is made up of molecules of different sizes. Scientists send this gas mixture through a tube of gel. Smaller molecules will travel through the gel faster, and bigger molecules will travel more slowly.

This is a machine for gas chromatography. The scientist has opened the machine to show the thin tube of gel inside. You can see the tube looping in a circle just in front of her hand.

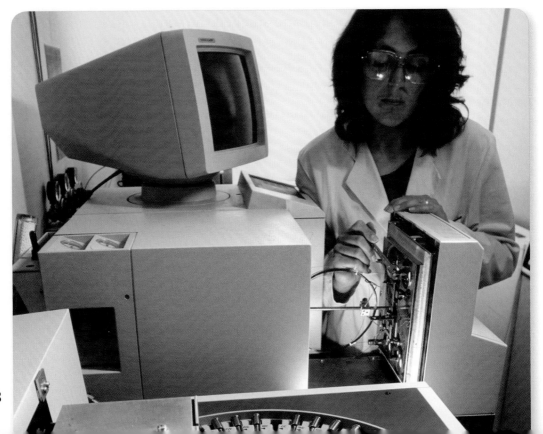

Each kind of molecule will come out of the tube at a different time, depending on how fast it travels. This lets the scientists study the molecules separately and identify each kind of molecule that was in the mixture. Identifying the molecules gives scientists lots of evidence to help them explain what a mixture is.

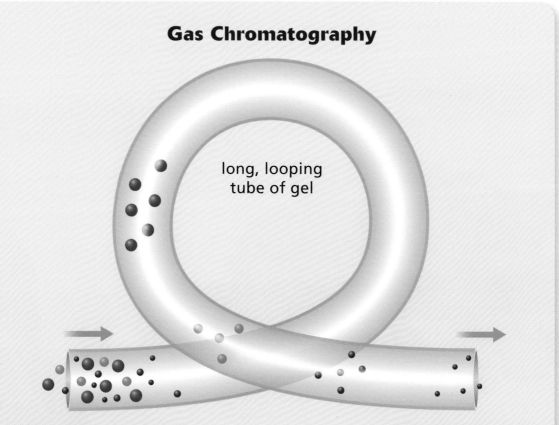

Gas Chromatography

long, looping
tube of gel

mixture of gas molecules
is pushed into the tube

smallest gas molecules
come out first

This diagram shows how gas chromatography separates molecules by size.

Using gas chromatography, scientists found evidence that the brown mixture had been a rich stew. They were able to identify molecules that matched different foods. Their evidence showed that the stew was made of roasted goat meat, lentils, honey, wine, and olive oil.

People threw a party for the scientists. Based on what the scientists had found out, a cook made a meal like the ancient feast. She used all the foods the scientists had identified.

meat

honey

lentils

These photos show some of
the foods scientists identified
in the brown mixture.

olive oil

Mixtures and Properties

The properties of the substances in a mixture are the keys to breaking it down. Sometimes scientists can separate a substance from a mixture by the size or shape of the substance's molecules. Scientists can often separate solids from liquids or liquids from gases. There are many other properties scientists can use to separate a mixture.

Mixtures are all around us. Scientists study mixtures in living things, in outer space, and deep underground. To understand and use a mixture, scientists often have to break it down. Breaking it down can be hard but also very important!

How could you separate pollution from the air?

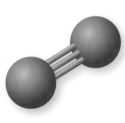

carbon dioxide
molecule

nitrogen
molecule

water
molecule

oxygen
molecule

Air is a mixture of gases. At the top of this page are models of different kinds of molecules that are found in air. The two molecules at the bottom of this page are kinds of air pollution. These substances are bad for living things. If you were a scientist trying to separate pollution molecules from the air, how might you do it? Can you think of properties you might use to separate the different substances in the air?

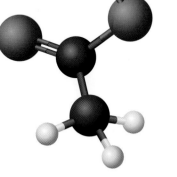

molecules from two
types of pollution

23

Glossary

acid: one of a group of substances, such as vinegar, that have properties such as being sour

atom: a tiny piece of matter that is too small to see

centrifuge: a tool that spins a mixture very fast to separate the parts

chromatography: a way to separate a mixture by passing it through a material

diagram: a simple illustration that explains how something works or what its parts are

evidence: clues that help explain something or answer a question

gas: matter that doesn't hold its shape, spreads out in all directions, and is usually invisible

identify: to figure out what something is or the group it belongs to

liquid: matter that doesn't hold its shape, flows, and makes puddles

matter: the stuff that things are made of

mixture: matter that is made of more than one substance

model: an object, a diagram, or a computer program that helps us understand something by making it simpler or easier to see

molecule: a group of atoms joined together in a particular way

plasma: the liquid part of blood

property: what you can observe or measure about something that helps you figure out what it is

solid: matter that holds its shape and doesn't make puddles

substance: matter that is made of only one kind of atom or molecule—for example, gold or water

temperature: how hot or cold something is